Anne Boleyn's Letter from the Tower

Sandra Vasoli

Anne Boleyn's Letter from the Tower

ISBN-13: 978-84-943721-5-5

M
MadeGlobal Publishing

For more information on
MadeGlobal Publishing, visit our website:
www.MadeGlobal.com

Contents

Cover Image: Anne Boleyn in the Tower by
Mohammad Rusdianto © 2015 MadeGlobal Publishing
After "Anne Boleyn in the Tower" by Edouard Cibot

FOREWORD

In November 2014 I planned to visit The British Library, London. My intent was to continue research as I wrote the second instalment of my fictional memoir of Anne Boleyn. The two-part novel, *Je Anne Boleyn*, highlights the fascinating relationship between Anne and Henry VIII, the great love of her life and her husband for a brief three years.

In preparation for the trip I spent considerable time thinking about what to request from the manuscripts room for the purpose of viewing original documents. I have found that the privilege of being permitted to touch and scrutinise original, handwritten archives is an invaluable experience – one that cannot be matched, no matter how much effort one devotes to a historical subject. In 2011, I was fortunate enough to examine the stunning *Book of Hours*, also in the British Library, which holds personal inscriptions from Anne and Henry. The experience was brilliant, and I was convinced, seeing this jewel-like volume in close proximity, that the story that has been told about the inscriptions – Anne and Henry quickly wrote them and exchanged the book in Mass – just didn't ring true. As a result, I discovered how much original documents have to say to their viewer.

Tantalised by the thought of poring over other intimate written exchanges between Henry and Anne, when I visited Rome in 2012 I determined to attempt to see the love letters that Henry wrote to Anne. Thanks to the preparation and efforts of very supportive friends and colleagues I was granted access to the Papal Archives and allowed several hours to study the letters in the original. The opportunity significantly changed how I regarded Anne and Henry's love affair, and forever changed my thinking about historical research.

I was extremely thoughtful about what I would most love to see, if possible. I read a short article about a letter Anne had written while she was held prisoner in the Tower of London, prior to her death, although history seems divided as to its legitimacy. The letter itself is so moving that I became absorbed by its story. I wanted to know everything I could about it, and discovered that it is housed in the British Library.

And so my decision was made.

Once in the manuscripts room at the library, I was assisted by the very helpful specialists and soon learned that the letter – the one considered the 'original' – is much too fragile, after having barely survived the Ashburnam House fire in 1731, to be handled. I was, however, given a remarkably detailed image of it, as well as other original, early documents, which mentioned or referred to it. That afternoon I saw a beautiful old copy of the letter written, I feel certain, by the Feathery Scribe, and two other intriguing entries that mentioned it. Spending time with these records, written so long ago, inhaling the powdery and mysterious aroma of age emanating from the parchment leaves of the volumes, observing the care with which information had been recorded and the spidery beauty of the script, all inspired me to pursue as complete a study of the letter as I could. In the past months, I have done just that.

There are as many opinions regarding how this letter was created as there are historians who have written about it. However, a good number do believe that Anne was its author. Simply the fact that so many records of the letter exist and have been debated and discussed by eminent authorities encourages me to think that this is a document that has something important to say. After studying Anne for many years, the emotional content of the letter and how it is expressed at its particular moment in time to her husband rings absolutely true to me as Anne revealing herself. Some say it is too well composed to be written by Anne. I contest that notion – especially considering that she probably knew it would be her final communication with her husband, and that her words might be preserved for the future. The language, the syntax, all is commensurate with that of the early- to mid-1500s. In seeking possibilities for the provenance of the document, I began by learning as much as I could about Sir Robert Bruce Cotton, in whose original collection within the library the manuscript exists. I studied the world of the seventeenth- and eighteenth-century antiquaries, including the eminent William Camden. And from that point on, the letter's derivation evolved.

In truth, we do not know unequivocally the origin of the scorched parchment in the library. And the world may never know who did compose those words without any remnant of doubt. But I believe it was Anne Boleyn, and I offer a credible scenario to contemplate.

While conducting my searches that day in the library, I spotted an old entry in a volume of handwritten parchment pages. The words that jumped out at me were towards the bottom of a page headed 'Memoirs of Queen Anne Boleyn'. I saw the phrase "the King acknowledges with great griefe …" I continued reading – and staring – and realised the passage referred to Henry's remorse over Anne's death. I had never heard or seen anything about this before, and I urgently scribbled everything I could in my notebook. Once home, I began to search for references to it, or for explanations of it. I have found enough information about this inscription to build on my fascination with the words and their provenance. There is a peculiar, but compelling possibility that the author of the passage did, in fact, have a personal contact with men who surrounded Henry while he was close to death. It's a captivating thread of history, and not one that has been widely disclosed. It is a fragment, though small and seemingly inconsequential, which deserves attention.

The ever enthralling story of Henry and Anne holds so many people in its grip the world over. Two charismatic, larger-than-life figures, whose short time together changed the world, and whose lives both came to tragic ends – this is the material for endless speculation and retelling of tales.

In my research, writing and preparation for publication, I have many generous people to thank for their willingness to help in any way possible.

My gratefulness always must extend first to my wonderful husband Tom, who engages readily and cheerfully in endless discussion about Henry and Anne.

I am enormously appreciative to Claire and Tim Ridgway. They are kind, supportive, encouraging and amazing sources of knowledge and creative energy. I am thrilled to be publishing with MadeGlobal.

To the assistants and the associates in the British Library, from the staff in the manuscripts room who answered many questions, helped with research, looked up dates, and steered me in proper directions, thank you. And thanks to those who accurately copied and sent the images I required and were so helpful in making sure I had exactly what I needed.

Huge thanks are in order to Cathy Giannascoli, who was critically helpful in her skilled translation of the important old French passage by André Thévet. Likewise, I extend my deep appreciation to Jon Pohlig whose wonderful interpretation of the Latin inscription by Melanchton, as copied by Bishop Kennett, enabled me to grasp its nuance.

I am absolutely indebted to Teri Fitzgerald for sharing her knowledge of Thomas Cromwell's son Gregory, and for the rewarding discussion about Ralph Sadler.

Thanks, as always, to Maria Maneos for her encouragement and advice.

In no small measure I am indebted to the warmth, interested encouragement and guidance of friends – so many of them in the wonderful virtual world of the love of Tudor history: Beth von Staats, Sarah Bryson, Deb Hunter, James Peacock, Natalie Grueninger, Adrienne Dillard, Gina Clark, Janet Ambrosi Wertman, Emma Wheatley, Debbie Brown, and Philippa Vincent-Gregory .

And finally, of course, I am always gratefully aware of how blessed I am for my family.

Thank you all.

Sandi Vasoli
Gwynedd Valley, PA
USA

Take away from History Why, How, and To What End things have been done, and whether the thing done hath succeeded according to Reason; and all that remains will rather be an idle Sport and Foolery, then a profitable instruction: and though for the present it may delight, for the future it cannot profit.

From *Polybius* as quoted by William Camden

Anne Boleyn's Tower Letter

Buried deep within the vaults of the British Library remains a compelling and mysterious letter, composed according to some by Queen Anne Boleyn to her husband Henry VIII. Its date is 6 May 1536 – four days after the queen was arrested at Greenwich and rowed to the Tower of London, not for the purpose of visiting a royal residence, but instead as a prisoner viciously accused of high treason.

The letter is poignant, courageous, noble and masterfully composed.

And for the past 475 years, its authenticity has been hotly debated.

This missive has been copied and published, much discussed and analysed by historians and authors throughout the centuries. It represents a significant moment in the annals of Britain and the world. Yet no one has unravelled its convoluted past.

Its content reveals a fervent proclamation of guiltlessness from a wife to her husband, along with her concern for his eternal soul, expressed in language both intimate and assertive. To read it is to gain a private glimpse into the spirit of a brave, articulate woman who knew she faced death.

Figure 1 - Hever portrait of Anne Boleyn © Tim Ridgway 2012

The marriage collapses

In the days and perhaps weeks leading to her arrest, Anne knew that her relationship with the king – once so wildly passionate and loving – had deteriorated, reaching an ominous nadir. Though there were numerous causes contributing to the marriage's demise, throughout that difficult time there remained hopeful signs of solidarity between Anne and Henry: a much anticipated trip planned for both to visit Calais; political positioning with European heads of state to reinforce Anne's place as Henry's legitimate wife and queen; and the continuation of their regular appearances together. Anne dauntlessly proclaimed to her ladies that she would soon become pregnant again following her tragic miscarriage in January 1536.

However, tension continued to build and Anne was required to cope with the recent devastating loss of a child while witnessing her husband's growing interest in a younger woman – a lady-in-waiting within her own household. Her distress must have been significant, and it undoubtedly prompted her to misjudge the wisdom of some of her actions and comments.

On 30 April at Greenwich, Anne was seen imploring Henry to turn from a window and speak with her. In a touchingly emotional gesture, she carried the nearly three-year-old Princess Elizabeth in her arms, and the king and queen were witnessed to have had a lengthy argument during which Anne could be seen desperately attempting to assuage Henry's anger. [1] It becomes

---

1   Ales, Alexander, Calendar of State Papers Foreign, Letter to Queen Elizabeth, 1558-1559.

apparent that Anne's attempt failed, the joint visit to Calais abruptly cancelled.

The following day, 1 May, was traditionally a celebratory day of jousts and feasting. Anne and Henry attended a tournament together, and though there is no specific record of the demeanour they shared, it does appear that Henry was in good spirits, smiling and being cordial to all. During the jousting competition, an unanticipated message was delivered to the king, for suddenly he stood and departed, taking with him just a few courtiers. Anne was left completely perplexed. Certainly she would have been apprehensive, for his actions did not bode well. Henry had left Greenwich to return to Whitehall without her.

Anne was never to see Henry again.

On Saturday 2 May, Queen Anne sat with her ladies watching a game of tennis. Her thoughts must have churned, considering the grim events of the previous two days. When an emissary arrived to tell Anne she was required on the king's orders to appear immediately before his privy counsellors, she undoubtedly made a mighty effort to quell her rising panic. Upon meeting with her uncle, the Duke of Norfolk, and two other council members, she was brusquely informed that she was under arrest for the crime of treason. She was accused of having had adulterous relations with several men. Her protestations of innocence were to no avail and she was escorted by barge to the Tower.

Once she arrived and was taken in as prisoner, she was met by the constable of the Tower, Sir William Kingston. He was to be her warden and jailer throughout the days that followed. Anne was housed in the queen's apartments in the royal palace, the same rooms within the Tower that Henry had refurbished for her prior to her coronation only three years previously. While her surroundings may have been comfortable, she was not to be consoled by the company of her dearest companions. Instead, the women assigned to serve and watch over her were those with whom she shared little closeness. Her initial discussions with

Kingston reveal her state of extreme anxiety. Anne alternated between tears and hysterical laughter as she perceived the horror of her circumstances. [2] During the excruciating days that ensued, Anne learned that her beloved brother George and her friends (and those of the king) Henry Norris, Francis Weston, William Brereton and the court musician Mark Smeaton were all imprisoned as well, charged with having had carnal relations with the queen.

The study of the precursors to, and the actual time of imprisonment of Anne Boleyn, is an extensive task and has been well documented and analysed (*see Resources*). But there are significant aspects that must be recounted to illuminate the context resulting in Anne's letter to Henry.

The relatively short span of thirty-six months since the marriage of Anne and Henry in January 1533 had been volatile, as an understatement. They had both endured years of fluctuating hope and great disappointment while Henry pursued a divorce from his first wife, Katharine of Aragon, in order to marry Anne, with whom he was deeply in love and who, he felt certain, would give him the son he needed and longed for. After being repeatedly refused the dispensation he sought from Pope Clement VII, and swept along by the tide of changing theological views, Henry freed himself from the restrictive doctrines imposed by the Church of Rome and the pope. Anne played a pivotal role in encouraging the king to establish himself as the head of the Church of England, thereby enabling his own decisions when it came to any and all matters pertaining to his realm. Amongst a small cadre of intellectuals and theologians who supported Henry's determination to divorce Katharine and marry Anne, and who shaped his philosophical arguments in defence of that decision, was Thomas Cranmer, a Cambridge clerical scholar, soon to become the Archbishop of Canterbury. The other decisive player in that drama was Thomas Cromwell.

---

2 Strype, John, *Ecclesiastical Memorials Under the Reign of King Henry VIII King Edward VI and Queen Mary I,* Vol I, 1816, p 447.

Cromwell, having risen through wit, ability and determination from the most meagre of beginnings, travelled in his youth to Italy, France and the Low Countries, working, learning and gaining skill in multiple languages. By 1515 he had returned to England where he became a part of the household of Cardinal Thomas Wolsey, who was young King Henry VIII's trusted cleric and advisor. He rose within Wolsey's employ, and by 1529 had become the lord chancellor's personal secretary, and had caught the attention of the king. His standing as an efficient and detail-oriented statesman and lawyer allowed him to survive the downfall of his mentor, Wolsey. By 1530, Cromwell was appointed by the king to his privy council. It was around then that Cromwell began to work tirelessly to advance the King's Great Matter – a divorce from Katharine and a subsequent marriage to Anne Boleyn. His dedication to this pursuit won him the king's favour.

Anne and Cromwell shared ideology concerning the advent of the new religion. This commonality, and also the fact that the keenly astute politician Cromwell recognised the ascendant power held by the Boleyn family, encouraged an alliance between Cromwell and Anne. Each provided impetus to the other's position at Court, while reinforcing the advancing reforms of the church. Cromwell handled a myriad of varied details in the daily lives of Henry and Anne: he was the chief organiser of Anne's elaborate coronation ceremony of June 1533, he played a key role in the management of the nursery of the infant Princess Elizabeth; he was master of the jewel house amongst other duties, all while providing legal counsel on the complicated politics of the day. Notably, he crafted and provided the enforcement to Henry's requirement that all of his subjects swear an oath recognising Anne as their queen. This role, as enforcer, revealed Cromwell's willingness to take brutal action when needed, since several of Henry's formerly closest advisers, including Thomas More and John Fisher, refused the oath. They

Figure 2 - Portrait of Thomas Cromwell, wearing the Garter collar, after Hans Holbein the Younger, circa 1537

were both put to death as a result – Cromwell having seen to the process leading to their executions. [3]

But while many accounts of the collaboration between Anne and Cromwell report that they were close and shared friendship, the truth is likely considerably different. Anne remained wary, knowing that Cromwell was once a trusted protégé of her enemy, Cardinal Wolsey. And Cromwell was far too shrewd to offer an outright commitment to anyone – that is, to anyone but himself and his king. So, as the marriage, and the affinity between Henry and Anne was tested – first with the birth of Elizabeth instead of the hoped for son, then by Anne's subsequent miscarriages, along with the dearth of supporters for her queenship at home and abroad – Cromwell watched the king and queen fight and argue, then passionately make up. Their capricious pattern was not lost on Cromwell and he, along with many at Court, must have wondered how long the marriage would survive.

As queen, Anne took it upon herself to assume a newly vital position in matters of state – a direct result of her sharp intelligence, excellent education and her innate desire to be heard with a voice equally dynamic to those of the men who surrounded her. At times, Henry appeared proud of her abilities. But alternately he lashed out, reminding her of her place as his wife. Following England's break from the Church of Rome, a plan had been established to dissolve many of the Catholic monasteries throughout the land and plunder their riches. Anne and Cromwell disagreed markedly over how this exercise was to be conducted, and especially over the disposition of the resulting funds. Here we see a distinctly benevolent characteristic of Anne's in her desire to use the proceeds to support the poor and create a charitable endowment to underwrite education. [4] Cromwell, on

---

3   Elton, G.R., *Reform and Renewal: Thomas Cromwell and the Common Weal*; University of Chicago Press Cambridge, 1974.

4   Latymer, William, *Cronickille of Anne Bulleyne,* Camden Miscellany Vol 39, Royal Historical Society, 1990, p 56.

the other hand, felt that the money should be poured back into the diminishing coffers of the Crown. Cromwell knew that the only person who had a greater influence over the king than he himself was Anne. Jointly, Anne recognised Cromwell's leverage with Henry – it reminded her of her husband's former subjugation to Cardinal Wolsey, which she had fought to disjoin. The existence of each threatened the position of the other. And so the rivalry between Anne Boleyn and Thomas Cromwell grew.

Jane Seymour was the young lady-in-waiting who, through careful coaching by her powerful family and the conservative faction at Court who opposed Anne and the Boleyns, had attracted Henry's attention. The Seymours had always been supporters of Katharine of Aragon, and remained staunchly aligned with the Catholic Church of Rome. The Imperial ambassador to England, Eustace Chapuys, was a friend of the Seymours, and united with them against Anne and the Boleyns. Chapuys was an opponent of Anne's from her very first appearance as Henry's paramour. He served the Spanish king, who was the nephew of Katharine of Aragon, and he deeply resented Anne's usurping Katharine's role as queen. He was relentless in his guarded attacks on Anne and privately referred to her as The Concubine, even after her marriage to the king and her coronation.

It was against this unsettled backdrop that Anne's opponents began to coalesce. The Seymours courted the favour of Chapuys, promising their advocacy for the Lady Mary, Katharine and Henry's daughter, who had long since been banished from Court. Chapuys was receptive to their overtures and he established his plan to persuade Cromwell to join forces. Cromwell's view of the Lady Mary, and perhaps also his opinion of the ousted Queen Katharine, may have been more sympathetic than he had revealed. For these and other reasons Cromwell dangerously began to strengthen his relationship with Anne's foe, Eustace Chapuys.

In April 1536, Anne carried out a fateful tactic. She had been known in her years at Court as Henry's sweetheart to make missteps. Not a woman to meekly hold her tongue, she expressed what she thought – a trait that didn't always derive the desired conclusion. In this instance, she collaborated with her preacher and almoner John Skip, who was responsible for organising her charitable contributions as queen, in the construct of a sermon he gave at Mass. This particular Mass was held on Passion Sunday and was attended by a full congregation, including most of the Court. Skip proceeded, by skilful use of Scriptural allegory, to comment on the reform of the monasteries. His parable served to sharply criticise royal counsellors for their position, accusing them of greed and misappropriation of the treasures and land which would be released. His lecture heightened in its rancour and symbolically pointed directly to Thomas Cromwell.[5] In addition to creating a furore amongst the council and other nobility, this event caused a rift between Anne and Cromwell that was never repaired.

Two weeks later, Chapuys and Cromwell attended an audience with the king. Cromwell had committed to the Imperial ambassador that he would support the discussion Chapuys hoped would lead to a reinstatement of privileges for Lady Mary, and a re-establishment of friendly diplomacy between Henry and Chapuys' master, the emperor Charles V. On the contrary, Henry's wish was for Chapuys, at long last, to pay homage to Queen Anne, fully acknowledging her position. As the encounter became ever more truculent, Cromwell attempted to mediate, confident that he could soothe the king and bring him around to deliver the outcome Chapuys had anticipated. Instead, Henry loudly berated them both, demonstrating his obstinacy with no possibility of being swayed by Cromwell. Cromwell was visibly angered and extremely distressed by the encounter, and had to retire from the room to regain his composure.[6]

---

5   Ives, Eric, *The Life and Death of Anne Boleyn*, Blackwell Publishing, Oxford, UK, 2004, p 307.

6   Calendar of State Papers, Spain, Volume 5 Part 2, 1536-1538, pp. 85-104.

This decisive event proved to Cromwell that he was a true adversary of Anne's. Furthermore, he had by then aligned himself with Chapuys, a treacherous position in which to be, should Anne discover it. It became clear that Henry was not willing to abandon Anne and her daughter Elizabeth in favour of Mary, no matter how much influence Cromwell thought he had with the king.

Therefore, Thomas Cromwell, who had been emboldened beyond his position by the many accolades and rewards granted by his king, and by his long-standing ability to whisper in the king's ear and sway him, decided that Anne posed too great a risk for his position, his career, his financial status and, ultimately, for his life.

He determined that he must devise a plan to remove her.

It is documented that Cromwell, after the debacle of the meeting with Henry and Chapuys, claimed he had fallen ill and was confined to his residence. It is now widely believed that during those days of Easter in 1536, he hid in order to formulate his strategy to bring about the downfall of Anne Boleyn.

Cromwell knew that implicating Anne in a strictly political or theological argument would never have sufficient strength to encourage Henry's action against her. His needed to be a plan of cunning, and he would strike where Henry was most vulnerable: his sense of manhood. Anne was known for her enjoyment of courtly romance and flirtations, and often held festive entertainments in her chambers. Thomas's scheme centred on inflaming the jealousy between Anne and Henry, and would incorporate comments Anne had made along with her behaviour, which could now be called into question. Cromwell engaged the assistance of courtiers who were antagonistic towards Anne, one of whom was her own uncle, Thomas Howard, the Duke of Norfolk.

Individuals were questioned, stories were told.

On 30 April, just two weeks after the infamous meeting between the king, Cromwell and Chapuys, the young court musician Mark Smeaton was summoned to Cromwell's manor.

There, Cromwell himself interrogated Smeaton, possibly aided by force, until Smeaton confessed to having had sexual relations with the queen on three occasions. He was arrested, thrown into the Tower prison, and Anne's fall from grace began. [7]

---

7   Ives E.; *The Life and Death of Anne Boleyn*; p 325; Ridgway, Claire, *The Fall of Anne Boleyn: A Countdown*, MadeGlobal Publishing, 2012.

Anne's brave assertion

Robert Bruce Cotton was born in 1571 in Denton, Huntingdonshire in England, to Thomas and Elizabeth Cotton. The son of well-to-do parents, he was carefully educated and from early on in life acquired a love of reading, books, manuscripts and libraries. His early training was at Westminster School, where his study and passion for learning was influenced by the erudite antiquarian and historian William Camden. While at Westminster, Cotton started to study antiquary science, mentored by Camden. He was taught that a true antiquarian is not simply a historian, or an individual with a passion for history, but instead one who reveres, collects, preserves and develops historical perspectives derived from original documents. Cotton graduated with a Bachelor of Arts from Jesus College, Cambridge, in 1585, and then attended Middle Temple in 1589. [8]

Robert Cotton formed a lifelong friendship with William Camden, who was a revered scholar, writer and collector of rare documents. Under Camden's tutelage, at the early age of seventeen, Cotton began amassing his collection of rare and important documents, the dedication to which remained with him throughout his life. With Camden he was a founder of the Society of Antiquaries. He served as a member of parliament on several occasions, and was active in politics and governance. By the end of his life, his collection of manuscripts, letters and artefacts was impressive, and when he died in 1631, he left all in

---

8   Thrush, A. and Ferris, J. ed., *The History of Parliament: the House of Commons 1604-1629,* Cambridge University Press, 2010.

Figure 3 - Portrait of Robert Cotton,
attributed to Cornelis Janssens van Ceulen, circa 1626

the safe-keeping of his son and grandson. His grandson, Sir John Cotton, transferred the collection to the care and preservation of the nation, which was confirmed by an Act of Parliament in 1701. This marvellous collection formed the basis for the British Library, in which the compilation resides even today.[9]

On 23 October 1731, the collection of documents and priceless relics that comprised the Cotton Library was damaged significantly in a fire at Ashburnham House in London, where it was being temporarily stored. In the library were 958 manuscripts, and approximately 110 were ruined. Another 100 were severely damaged. These damaged documents, along with many burnt segments found in a warehouse in 1837 and determined to be part of the original Cotton collection, were subject to a restoration and stabilisation project. Although early attempts were clumsy, many documents that might otherwise have been entirely lost were salvaged, and remain in the British Library's archives. A double-sided letter, which is signed "Anne Boleyn" from "my doleful Prison the Tower, this 6th of May", scorched and ravaged by flames, is an item in that collection.[10]

Also in the Cotton Otho manuscripts (Robert Cotton catalogued his documents using names of Roman emperors from ancient times – Otho being one – and by grouping the manuscripts from A through E), adjacent to the damaged letter from Anne Boleyn are four of the five letters that the constable, William Kingston, wrote to Thomas Cromwell, on his orders, so that Cromwell might be fully informed of the queen's actions and state of mind while imprisoned. These letters, like Anne's, are charred and fragmented. Fortunately, Kingston's reports and the letter signed from Anne had been copied – perhaps numerous times – before the fire in 1731. It is due to the diligent work of

---

9   Richardson, R.C., "William Camden and the Re-Discovery of England", Trans. Leicestershire Archeological and Historical Society, 78, 2004.

10   Keynes, Simon," The Reconstruction of a Burnt Cottonian Manuscript", British Library articles, www.bl.uk; 1996.

antiquarians and their scribes that we know today the complete text of each of these six letters.

How, then, did Sir Robert Cotton come to hold the documents from Kingston to Thomas Cromwell, and the letter from the queen to her husband? And why is the derivation of the letter so important?

This is where the sleuthing becomes very challenging. Yet the answers, if they are to be discovered, are extremely meaningful, because if we can follow the provenance of these documents, it may reveal facts that support their authenticity. Most notable perhaps, the validity of Anne's letter in particular would provide additional evidence toward reinforcing her claim of innocence of the crimes for which she was indicted. It's interesting that the legitimacy of the letters from Kingston to Cromwell has not been called into question. It is Anne's that has confounded historians and scholars through the years. The Kingston letters indicate that they were presumably handed by Kingston himself to Cromwell, during Cromwell's several visits to the Tower to assess the situation. While there he saw Kingston, but there is no documentation to imply that Cromwell ever saw or spoke with Anne. It is probable, though, that he provided Kingston with a reply to Anne's plea to be allowed to see Henry. The answer: unequivocally, no. [11]

Once ensconced in the Tower, attended by ladies not of her choosing or liking, Anne's every word was monitored and her behaviour noted and recorded by William Kingston. Within two days of her arrest and imprisonment, she learned the shocking and horrible news that Francis Weston, Henry Norris, William Brereton and her brother George had been accused along with her and were likewise imprisoned. She anguished at the thought of her mother being informed of the fate of two of her three children, and grieved that her poor lady mother would die of sorrow. She asked for, and received, Holy Communion, thereby

---

11   Burnet, Gilbert, *Historie of the Reformation of the Church of England*, Part One, London, 1679, pp 203 – 205.

demonstrating her innocence before God. And all the while she must have hoped and prayed that she would have a chance to see and speak with her husband, so that she might work her magic with Henry as she once had, restore his love for her and convince him that she had ever been a devoted wife to him and him alone.

It is not difficult to imagine that once her hopes of an audience with the king were crushed, she desired – and probably insisted upon – the opportunity to write to him. It would be entirely unlike Anne to meekly shrink from having her say. She needed to express herself to her husband, and she would do so in writing if not personally. In fact, Kingston himself references Anne's desire to compose a letter, and she asks Kingston if he will be the messenger who will deliver it to Cromwell, presumably with the belief that he would then convey it to the king:

> I shalle desyre you to bayre a letter from me [...] [to Master] Secretory. And then I sayd, Madam, telle it me by [word of mouth, and I] wille do it. And so gaf me thankes, sayinge I ha[ve much marvel] that the Kynges conselle commes not to me. [12]

Cromwell would have been informed by Kingston that Anne intended to compose a letter. Whether he believed her desire to communicate with the king would be prudent in terms of his own personal strategy or not, he would certainly have realised the inadvisability of refusing her that privilege. She was, after all, the queen, and the king her husband. Thus, the letter was formulated and written.

It is unknown if, on 6 May, Anne put her own hand to quill and parchment. She may have. Conversely, it seems more likely that she would have been compelled to dictate her well thought out and carefully composed remarks to someone who scribed the letter for her. What we do know today is that the

---

12   Letters and Papers, Foreign and Domestic, Henry VIII, Volume 10, January-June 1536; 3 May, Otho, C. x. 222.
B. M. Singer's Cavendish, ii. 220. Ellis, I. Ser. ii. 56

document that is in the Cotton collection in the British Library is not in Anne's handwriting. Although there are few examples of Anne's original writing, it is clear, upon observation, that her script does not match this letter's. That being the case, might it be the writing of one of the ladies who served her in the Tower? It's possible, though not likely. The writing is not that of Cromwell, nor does it match William Kingston's either, so he did not scribe for Anne. Although the scrivener is unknown, the letter's message is strong and unmistakable:

> Sir, Your Grace's Displeasure and my Imprisonment are Things so strange unto me, as what to Write, or what to Excuse, I am altogether ignorant. Whereas you send unto me (willing me to confess a Truth, and to obtain your Favour) by such an one whom you know to be my ancient professed Enemy; I no sooner received this Message by him, than I rightly conceived your Meaning; and if, as you say, confessing a Truth indeed may procure my safety, I shall with all Willingness and Duty perform your Command.

> But let not your Grace ever imagine that your poor Wife will ever be brought to acknowledge a Fault, where not so much as a Thought thereof proceeded. And to speak a truth, never Prince had Wife more Loyal in all Duty, and in all true Affection, than you have ever found in Anne Boleyn, with which Name and Place I could willingly have contented my self, if God, and your Grace's Pleasure had been so pleased. Neither did I at any time so far forget my self in my Exaltation, or received Queenship, but that I always looked for such an Alteration as now I find; for the ground of my Preferment being on no surer Foundation than your Grace's Fancy, the least Alteration, I knew, was fit and sufficient to draw that Fancy to some other Subject. You have chosen me, from a low Estate, to be your Queen and Companion,

far beyond my Desert or Desire. If then you found me worthy of such Honour, Good your Grace let not any light Fancy, or bad Councel of mine Enemies, withdraw your Princely Favour from me; neither let that Stain, that unworthy Stain of a Disloyal Heart towards your good Grace, ever cast so foul a Blot on your most Dutiful Wife, and the Infant Princess your Daughter:

Try me good King, but let me have a Lawful Trial, and let not my sworn Enemies sit as my Accusers and Judges; yea, let me receive an open Trial, for my Truth shall fear no open shame; then shall you see, either mine Innocency cleared, your Suspicion and Conscience satisfied, the Ignominy and Slander of the World stopped, or my Guilt openly declared. So that whatsoever God or you may determine of me, your Grace may be freed from an open Censure; and mine Offence being so lawfully proved, your Grace is at liberty, both before God and Man, not only to execute worthy Punishment on me as an unlawful Wife, but to follow your Affection already settled on that Party, for whose sake I am now as I am, whose Name I could some good while since have pointed unto: Your Grace being not ignorant of my Suspicion therein.

But if you have already determined of me, and that not only my Death, but an Infamous Slander must bring you the enjoying of your desired Happiness; then I desire of God, that he will pardon your great Sin therein, and likewise mine Enemies, the Instruments thereof; and that he will not call you to a strict Account for your unprincely and cruel usage of me, at his General Judgment-Seat, where both you and my self must shortly appear, and in whose Judgment, I doubt not, (whatsover the World may think of me) mine Innocence shall be openly known, and sufficiently cleared.

My last and only Request shall be, That my self may only bear the Burthen of your Grace's Displeasure, and that it may not touch the Innocent Souls of those poor Gentlemen, who (as I understand) are likewise in strait Imprisonment for my sake. If ever I have found favour in your Sight; if ever the Name of Anne Boleyn hath been pleasing in your Ears, then let me obtain this Request; and I will so leave to trouble your Grace any further, with mine earnest Prayers to the Trinity to have your Grace in his good keeping, and to direct you in all your Actions. From my doleful Prison the Tower, this 6th of May.

Your most Loyal and ever Faithful Wife,

Anne Boleyn [13]

Upon reading the missive, one is struck by its tenor of familiarity that which, even in the direst of circumstances, is emblematic of the close relationship between husband and wife. Her opening line, *"Sir, Your Grace's Displeasure and my Imprisonment are things so strange unto me, as what to write, or what to excuse, I am altogether ignorant"*, is reminiscent of arguments known to couples throughout the ages. She then chastises him for having allowed her to be confronted by her uncle, Norfolk, who was antagonistic towards her.

In the second paragraph she confirms an understanding that her position as queen was not due to birth of royal standing, as were most other European princesses. Instead, she acknowledges that their foundation was based upon love – a very unusual occurrence in royal marriages of the day. She accedes to the notion that the preservation of her role as his wife and queen was dependent on his continued devotion to her. She then delivers a blow by telling him she is well aware that

---

13   British Library, Cotton Otho C X fol. 232 r

Figure 4 - Burnt Fragment of the letter
© 01/09/2015 The British Library Board, Cotton Otho CX f232r

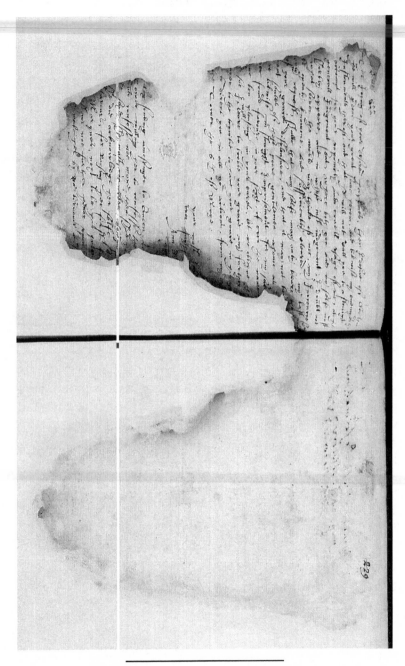

Figure 5 - Burnt Fragment of the letter
© 01/09/2015 The British Library Board, Cotton Otho CX f232v

his "Fancy" has turned to "some other subject". She is quick, though, to express her humility, recalling that he chose her from a "low Estate". She pointedly refers to herself, in the letter as well as in her signature, as "Anne Boleyn, with which name and place I could willingly have contented myself". This statement in particular is remarkable. Here she reminds him that she was simply Anne Boleyn when they met, and *he* pursued *her* relentlessly until she capitulated and became his queen. She now addresses him as that self-same woman. There is, in this very point, a subtlety of meaning expressed that seems impossible – and improbable – for a forger to invent.

Further on, Anne is true to the piquant nature for which she was well known. She asserts that if he has already decided she is guilty of his "Infamous Slander", and her death will "bring you the enjoying of your desired happiness", then she hopes for Henry's sake that God will pardon him for his "unprincely and cruel usage", for, as she admonishes him – they will both shortly appear before God and be subject to His judgement. She adds the final jolt: she is confident God will know her to be innocent and she will be sufficiently cleared. Her implication is strong – as for Henry? She worries for the salvation of his eternal soul due to his "great Sin".

Anne continues by agonising for the men she knows have been unjustly imprisoned on her behalf. In this paragraph one can feel her anguish. She begs Henry to be lenient with them if ever he loved her, exactly as a woman would do when beseeching a man with whom she had been intimate. Finally, she closes by affirming herself – not as queen – but as Henry's loyal and ever faithful wife, Anne Boleyn.

The characteristics displayed in this very personal, highly charged message reflect everything we have come to know about Anne and the way she conducted herself. Honest, outspoken, unafraid to speak her mind. Heedless as to what might be considered proper in such desperate circumstances, she told Henry what she wanted him to know. And she did so as wife to husband, not from queen to king.

The letter flows onto the opposite side of the single page. On the reverse, positioned about an inch below Anne's signature, there is an intriguing postscript. This passage has been damaged significantly, but at least two antiquaries were able to record the words before they were lost. The message is as follows:

> The King sending a message to Queen Anne, being prisoner in the Tower, willing her to confess the Truth, she said she could confess no more than she had already spoken. And she said she must conceal nothing from the King, to whom she did acknowledge herself so much bound for so many favours, for raising her first from a mean woman to be a Marquess, next to be his Queen, and now, seeing he could bestow no further honour upon her on earth, for purposing to make her, by martyrdom, a saint in heaven.[14]

The handwriting of both the body of the letter and the footnote is identical. As for the timing of these two messages, one might realistically imagine that the letter from Anne to the king had been composed and drafted, but before it was sent from the Tower, a message arrived from the king demanding that Anne confess the truth. The scribe then, in the presence of Constable Kingston, recorded Anne's response, which she desired to be sent along with her initial letter to Henry.

---

14   Ibid.

The letter's mystery

Thus we are left with a great enigma.

If Anne created this composition, did she actually place a quill to paper and write? If so, what happened to that document? If not, what is the background of the letter that is now part of the Cotton Library?

As is most often the case when we reconstruct history, there are undeniable facts available to us, and gaps that must be filled to recreate and understand an event. The circumstances resulting in this letter fit the pattern. We have clues and some solid evidence, but to present a convincing case for a logical conclusion we must employ reasonable deduction. Therefore, we can construct a plausible scenario with the information that is accessible.

Let us presume that Cromwell and Kingston did not allow Anne to write a private message to her husband. Cromwell was necessarily consumed by his role as enforcer. At that point, his very life depended upon his plan's success, and it would have behoved him to ensure nothing went amiss with Anne's imprisonment, trial and sentence. It was important that he knew precisely what Anne said to the king and a sealed letter would entail too much risk. Instead, and as a compromise, they may have permitted her to dictate her thoughts while a scribe, under the watchful eye of Kingston, placed her words on the parchment, which would then have been handed to Cromwell for intended delivery to the king. Cromwell, upon receipt of Anne's scribed letter, read it and made the decision – admittedly a treacherous one, but at that volatile time, what action was not without peril? – to hide the letter amongst his most personal belongings, ensuring that Henry would never see what his wife had expressed to him. Were Henry to read her entreaty and be moved by it, the possibility was too great that he would reverse his decision, and that chance was untenable for Cromwell. He was, after all, a lawyer, and one who valued efficiency to achieve an end result. He was also an avid student of the Machiavellian principles that espoused that clever scheming was required to manage effectively, even if it meant disposing of kindness or morality.[15] These characteristics might have lent themselves to his determination never to provide the king with his wife's last communication. Cromwell's training and practice in the legal arena informed his decision not to destroy the document. Evidence must never be destroyed, but rather manoeuvred to one's advantage to obtain the desired outcome. And so, hidden within his most private papers, the scribed original letter lay for at least four years.

Several very reliable accounts report that the parchment that became part of the Cotton collection was "said to be found among the papers of Cromwell then Secretary". [16]

The Stowe Collection of manuscripts, also held in the British Library, includes a copy of the original letter. This may well be the earliest known copy and it is part of a volume entitled *Collection of Letters of Noble Personages*. At the top of the page is written:

> Queen Anne Bulling
> For King Henry the 8 ffounde amongst Cromwell's papers [17]

---

15 Cavendish, George, *The Life of Thomas Wolsey*, ed. Ellis, F. S., Kelmscott Press, London, 1893; and T. M. Parker, "Was Thomas Cromwell a Machiavellian?", The Journal of Ecclesiastical History, Volume 1, Issue 01 , April 1950 pp 63 -75, published online by Cambridge University Press, 25 Mar 2011.

16 Lord Herbert of Cherbury, *The Life and Raigne of King Henry the Eighth*, Thomas Whitaker, London; 1649, p 382.

17 British Library; Stowe MS 151.

A later copy of the letter, source unknown, states "found amongst Cromwell's papers".

The historian and theologian Gilbert Burnet (b 1643 – d 1718) states: "The copy I take it from, lying among Cromwell's other papers, makes me believe it was truly written by her." [18] So we may be fairly certain that the letter now in the Cotton collection was discovered by someone searching Thomas Cromwell's papers after he, too, was beheaded for treason in 1540. How long after his death was this document, along with the letters from Kingston chronicling Anne's time in the Tower, found? We don't have any direct evidence to tell us. Who disclosed the letters and why did Cromwell hold them in private? Again, nothing written by any of the contemporaries of Cromwell's, or the early antiquaries, gives us a definitive indication of the letter's earliest provenance.

Let us examine the knowledge we do have in the hope that we might draw a believable conclusion.

The library's Stowe collection contains the first known handwritten copy of the original letter. The British Library references this collection as representing various transcripts written in three professional hands, one being that of the Feathery Scribe. The collection is dated as being completed prior to 1628. The transcribed letter, from "Anne Bulling", is in fact the work of the Feathery Scribe.[19]

Roy Flannagan explains that the "Feathery Scribe was an anonymous copyist who has, in recent years, been so named because of the light, wispy style of his script. He was one of the most prominent and most easily distinguishable of the many copyists who flourished in London in the 1620s and 1630s. He was master of a consistently accomplished script, almost pure secretary but for the occasional adoption of italic for names

---

18   Burnet, *A History of the Reformation of the Church of England*.

19   British Library Online, *Explore Archives and Manuscripts*,
      Stowe MS 151.

or headings."[20] He was prolific, and worked for prominent statesmen and nobles of his day.

Who might have commissioned the Feathery Scribe to copy and preserve Anne's letter? As Beal states in his study of the scribe, "Among the Feathery Scribe's clients were almost certainly various MPs, including the ubiquitous collector Sir Robert Cotton." Another eminent figure whose documents the Feathery Scribe is said to have copied was William Cecil, Lord Burghley.[21] Therefore, we know that someone of importance contracted the Feathery Scribe to reproduce the letter in order to preserve the words for posterity, directly from the one found in Cromwell's papers, prior to 1628.

In the years following the discovery of the letter, distinguished historians and antiquarians have made specific reference to it in their writings. Some actually saw the original, others did not. All had an opinion of it, however. One of the first chroniclers to mention the letter was Lord Herbert of Cherbury (1583-1648), in *The Life and Raigne of King Henry the Eighth*. This work was published in 1649. Herbert says: "after which another Letter in her name, but no Originall coming to my hand, from more than one good part, I thought fit to Transcribe here, without other Credit yet then that it is said to be founde among the papers of Cromwell then Secretary, and for the rest seems antient and consonant to the matter in question." He then reprints her text, which is followed by this comment: "but whether this Letter were elegantly written by her, or any else heretofore, I know as little, as what answer might be made thereunto". [22]

Bishop Gilbert Burnet (1643 – 1715), a Scotsman, was a highly regarded intellectual, fluent in numerous languages and knowledgeable in philosophy and theology. He was passionate

---

20   Flannagan, Roy,"Review of *In Praise of Scribes*",Early Modern Literary Studies 5.1, May, 1999.

21   Ibid.

22   Lord Herbert of Cherbury, *Life and Raigne of King Henry the Eighth*.

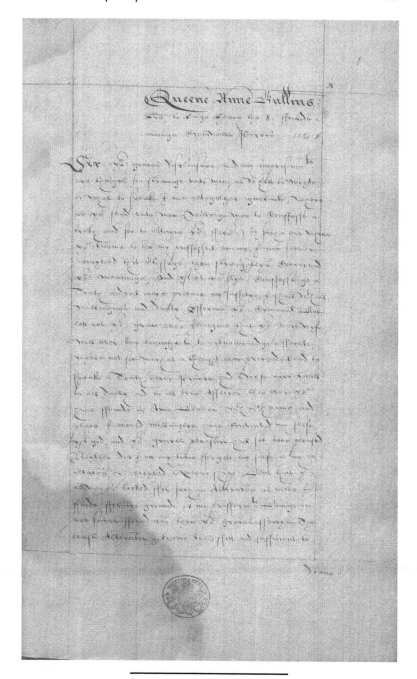

Figure 6 - © 01/09/2015 The British Library Board, Stowe MS 151

about history and had a great respect for original documents. In 1679, he published the first of three volumes of *The History of the Reformation of the Church of England*. Volume I recounts events during the reign of Henry VIII, and Burnet devotes numerous pages to the downfall of Queen Anne Boleyn, who he describes as a "good woman" and "of a cheerful temper". His notation about the Tower Letter is as follows:

> Yet, in a Letter that she wrote to the King from the Tower [...] she pleaded her innocence in a strain of so much wit, and moving passionate eloquence, as perhaps can scarce be paralleled, certainly her spirits were much exalted when she wrote it, for it is a pitch above her ordinary style. Yet the copy I take it from lying among Cromwell's other papers, makes me believe it was truly written by her. [23]

Next we read John Strype's (1643 – 1737) entry in his *Ecclesiastical Memorials and the Reformation of it and the Emergencies of the Church of England under King Henry VIII, King Edward VI and Queen Mary I*. He mentions the letter, quoting the addendum in which Anne refers to Henry making her a saint in heaven. Strype's *Memorials* was published in 1833. [24]

Sir Henry Ellis (1777 – 1869) was a well-known scholar, whose lifelong interest in books and documents led him to positions of authority at the Bodleian Library at Oxford, and ultimately to his role as head librarian at the British Museum. He was an avid antiquarian, holding the position of secretary in the London Society of Antiquaries for some time. With the access he had to precious documents, he published multiple volumes of *Original Letters Illustrative of English History*. In 1825, he included in Volume II some commentary about the letter in question. He states:

---

23   Burnet, *History of the Reformation*, Book III, p 206.

24   Strype, *Ecclesiastical Memorials*, p 452.

Anne Boleyn's last memorable letter to Henry the Eighth is [...] universally known as one of the finest compositions in the English language, and is only mentioned here, to obviate a notion which has gone abroad against it as a forgery. The Original, it is believed, is not remaining now, but the Copy of it preserved among Lord Cromwell's papers together with Sir William Kyngston's Letters, is certainly in a hand-writing of the time of Henry the Eighth: and Sir William Kyngstons evidence will show that Anne was too closely guarded to allow of anyone concerting such a letter with her. That it rises in style above Anne Boleyn's other compositions cannot be disputed, but her situation was one which was likely to rouse a cultivated mind; and there was a character of nature in the Letter, a simplicity of expression, and a unity of feeling, which it may be doubted whether Genius itself may have feigned. [25]

James Froude (1818 – 1894) was an English writer and publisher. Over a period spanning two decades he wrote *The History of England from the Fall of Wolsey to the Defeat of the Spanish Armada*. His writing has been criticised as being overly emotional rather than factual, and he referred to Anne's imprisonment, and the letter, in the following passages:

Instead of acknowledging any guilt in herself, she perhaps retaliated upon the king in the celebrated letter which has been thought a proof both of her own innocence, and of the conspiracy by which she was destroyed. This letter also, although at once so well known and of so dubious authority, it is fair to give entire. [he reprints the text] [...] This letter is

---

25 Ellis, Henry, Original Letters, *Illustrative of English History*, Vol II, Thomas Davison, Whitefriars, London 1815, p 53.

most affecting; and although it is better calculated to plead the queen's cause with posterity than with the king, whom it could only exasperate, yet if it is genuine it tells (so far as such a composition can tell at all) powerfully in her favour. On the same page of A second requisition to confess from the king, and a second refusal.

The tone of the queen's answers not what it ought to have been, even on her own showing. The manuscript, carrying the same authority, and subject to the same doubt, is a fragment of another letter, supposed to have been written subsequently, and therefore in answer to a second invitation to confess. In this she replied again, that she could confess no more than she had already spoken; that she might conceal nothing from the king, to whom she did acknowledge herself so much bound for so many favours; for raising her first from a mean woman to be a marchioness; next to be his queen; and now, seeing he could bestow no further honours upon her on earth, for purposing by martyrdom to make her a saint in heaven, This answer also was unwise in point of worldly prudence; and I am obliged showing to add, that the tone which was assumed, both in this and in her first letter, was unbecoming (even if she was innocent of actual sin) in a wife who, on her own showing, was so gravely to blame. It is to be remembered that she had betrayed from the first the king's confidence; and, as she knew at the moment at which she was writing, she had never been legally married to him. [26]

In the 1850s, Agnes Strickland wrote and published *Lives of the Queens of England: From the Norman Conquest*. It

---

26   Froude, James, *History of England from the Fall of Wolsey to the Death of Elizabeth*, Vol II, Scribner, New York, 1872, p 443.

was a colossal task and her research is recognised as well-done. While her style of writing was not acknowledged as having been particularly excellent, she strove to do her subjects justice. She addresses both the 6 May letter and the addendum in which Anne thanks Henry for raising her to the level of martyr in such a way that the author assumed them as fact. She also, interestingly, mentions that the addendum was notated by either Cromwell or his secretary.[27]

It is clear that the pre-eminent experts throughout the sixteenth to the nineteenth centuries treated the letter in a way that gave credence to its historical significance. It is worth noting that none offer information on how the Kingston and Boleyn letters were discovered, or by whom, nor do they comment on how these documents became part of the Cotton library collection. But at least most of them believe that, although not written in Anne's hand, the letter is an authentic composition by the imprisoned queen.

---

27 Strickland, Agnes, *Lives of the Queens of England*, Vols 4 and 5, Lea and Blanchard, 1851, p 208.

The bequest of Thomas Cromwell

In a catastrophic turn of events, in the early afternoon of 10 June 1540, Thomas Cromwell, newly raised as the Earl of Essex, was arrested and accused of heresy and treason. Cromwell had been perhaps more involved than ever in endless details involving state and personal matters on behalf of the king. Admittedly, his most recent work in attempting to cultivate a relationship and marriage between the king and the German princess Anne of Cleves had not gone well. Yet his own arrest and imprisonment must have been as much a shock to him as had Anne's to her four years prior. Cromwell, in pleading for his life, wrote an impassioned letter to Henry. What an ironic twist of fate! It is said, though not proven, that Henry had the letter read aloud to him three times and almost yielded to its entreaty. He decided, though, against it, and Cromwell's fate, just like Anne's, was sealed. He was taken prisoner to remain in the Tower until his death by beheading on 28 July. During his time in prison, Cromwell leaned on his closest and perhaps most trusted companion, his personal secretary, Ralph Sadler. Sadler's position and stature was due to his association with and tutelage by Thomas Cromwell. It was Sadler whom Cromwell relied upon to deliver directly to the king the letter in which he begged for mercy. In 1529, Cromwell had appointed Sadler as the executor of his will, and he was designated as a beneficiary of part of the estate. [28]

This point, in particular, is of critical importance.

---

28   http://www.historyofparliamentonline.org/volume/1509-1558/ member/sadler-ralph-1507-87.

Figure 7 - Ralph Sadler,
Portrait of an Unidentified Man by Hans Holbein the Younger
Royal Collection, Windsor Castle, 1535

As executor, Sadler would have been entitled to know the content of Cromwell's estate. It is possible that Sadler knew the whereabouts of the letter Cromwell had hidden from the king – Anne's letter.

It is likely, even probable, that Cromwell had Sadler engage the appropriate scribe for the task of writing Anne's letter. And it may well have been Ralph Sadler who, with Kingston, sat in Anne's suite of rooms in the Tower and oversaw the transaction of the letter being written by the scribe.

Pondering who Cromwell would have entrusted when he was told that Anne wished to send a communiqué to Henry, his confidante and loyal secretary Ralph Sadler is an obvious choice. We know that Cromwell did not make an appearance to visit Anne while she was imprisoned ("I ha[ve much marvel] that the Kynges conselle commes not to me")[29] and the pieces begin to fit knowing that a message from the king was delivered to Anne demanding her true confession. This royal directive would have been conveyed via one source only – and that would have been Cromwell. Since he did not deliver it in person, it would only have been carried by his closest associate, one who would understand the dire implications of both the request and the response. Sadler would have witnessed the scribe adding Anne's reply to Henry's demand. He would have assured her that the entire letter, with the addendum, would be promptly delivered to Cromwell and hence to the king. Sadler may then have taken the letter to Cromwell, who tucked it away with his private belongings with no intent of its dispatch to Henry, who likely never knew of its existence. It is not a far leap of imagination, then, to think that Sadler may have known, or have been told, where Anne's letter, accompanied by Kingston's, were kept, and importantly, that he could be depended upon to keep the secret.

Therefore, when Cromwell's belongings were seized upon his arrest, it is not improbable that Sadler knew of the letter's location and was able to save it from being taken by the Crown.

---

29   British Library, Cotton MS Otho C X fol. 222.

For how long did Ralph Sadler hold the letters after Cromwell died? There is no way of knowing, if indeed this is true. But we can develop a credible account of their disposition.

The next step in the letter's provenance seems equally probable. It is well-documented that Ralph Sadler and William Cecil, Lord Burghley (1520 – 1598), were close friends and colleagues. Burghley had relegated Sadler with handling closely guarded secrets as Elizabeth was being positioned to ally with the Protestants of Scotland. Letters between William Cecil and Sadler attest to their collaboration on matters of state as well as their friendship. At some point after 1540, the letter Anne composed may have been given by Ralph Sadler to William Cecil.

Cecil was a man who loved books and owned, as well as collected, important documents. He was responsible for Elizabeth I's most personal papers throughout their lives, even into their later years.[30] He was her secretary, her champion and her advisor all the years of her queenship. He knew her well and cared for her greatly. It seems believable, then, that the fervent letter her mother wrote to her father was shown to Elizabeth.

Many believe, even though she did not speak publicly of her, there are strong indicators that Elizabeth held her mother close to her heart and in high regard. Knowledge of the letter Anne composed while awaiting death in the Tower may have been one more heartrending detail in the impression Elizabeth maintained of the mother she scarcely remembered.

Perhaps Queen Elizabeth commanded William Cecil, or it may have been the man himself who determined the importance of preserving the words Anne composed. It is suggested that William Cecil paid due to the letter's legacy by arranging a commission for a copy of the letter to be made, thereby ensuring if the original was lost, a rendition would remain. The notion was prescient because, as we know, the original version was in

---

30   Nares, Edward, *Memoirs of the Life and Administration of the Right Honourable William Cecil, Lord Burghley,* Saunders and Otley, London, 1828, p 181.

Figure 8 - William Cecil, Lord Burghley
Victorian Etching from Cassell's History of England

fact almost lost in the Ashburnam fire, over 100 years later. Today, a copy made by the Feathery Scribe at some time in the early 1600s remains intact as a part of the Stowe collection of documents.

Among the friends and very close colleagues of William Cecil, Lord Burghley, was the antiquarian William Camden (1551 -1623). Burghley thought enough of Camden that he commended him to write a history of the reign of his beloved Queen Elizabeth. Camden spent some years labouring over this treatise, which was entitled *Annales Rerum Gestarum Angliae et Hiberniae Regnate Elizabetha*. Originally written in Latin, the biographical and historical account was translated and then published in English in 1628. He did not complete the commitment, though, until after both his sponsors, Burghley and Elizabeth, had died. A man dedicated to the preservation of history in its truest recitation, as told through genuine artefacts, Camden states:

> Mine own writings and remembrances I searched over, who though I have been a studious regarder of venerable Antiquity, yet as one not altogether carelesse of late and fresh matters, I have seen, observed, and received many things from my Ancestors, and credible persons, which have beene present at the handling of matters, and such as have been addicted to the parties on both sides in this contrariety of Religion. All which I have with the Ballance of mine owne Judgement (such as it is) weighed and examined, lest I should at any time through beguiling credulity incline to that which is false. For the love of Truth, as it hath beene the onely spurre unto me to undertake this worke, so hath it also beene my onely scope and aime. Which truth to take from history, is nothing else but to plucke out the eyes of the beautifullest living creature, and in

stead of wholesome nourishment, to offer a draught of poyson to the Readers mindes. [31]

Burghley provided and also bequeathed a great store of his precious and private library of documents to Camden to enable his work, and because he knew William Camden would respect and protect them for the future. It would follow that included in the collection left to Camden upon Burghley's death in 1598 was the packet of letters written by William Kingston along with the letter Anne composed. It seems almost indisputable that both men, who knew and respected documents that were true witness to history, believed this letter was credible, legitimate and very worthy of immense care and preservation.

William Camden, as mentioned before, was the mentor, tutor and lifelong friend of Robert Bruce Cotton:

> I am beholden to that most excellent man Sir Robert Cotton, Knight and Baronet, who hath with great cost, and successefull industry, furnished himselfe with most choice store of matter of History and Antiquity (for from his light, he hath most willingly given great light to me). So (Reader) if I shall in any thing helpe or delight thee in this behalfe, thou art most worthily to give him thankes for the same. [32]

It has been well-recorded that Camden left a significant bequest to Cotton – his compilation of documents, letters, epistles and books. Camden's store of collected works therefore became a keystone of Cotton's library.[33]

---

31 Camden, William, *Historie of the Most Renowned and Victorious Princesse Elizabeth Late Queen of England*, Benjamin Fisher, London, 1630, Foreward.

32 Ibid.

33 http://www.celm-ms.org.uk/introductions/CamdenWilliam.html

Figure 9 - Portrait of William Camden, engraved by R.White,
front piece to *Camden's Britannia*.

The recordings made by William Kingston along with Anne's Tower Letter, we may reasonably assume, were a part of the inheritance Robert Cotton received from William Camden.

Anne's letter was an important specimen in the Cotton Manuscripts.

The Cotton Manuscripts comprised one of the foundations of the British Library upon its establishment in 1753.

Thus, in the considered opinion of this author, within the British Library today remain the final words from Anne Boleyn to Henry VIII.

Henry's 'Great Griefe'

It is heartbreaking to think that Anne's letter may never have been seen by Henry. She may or may not have believed her words would reverse his cruel decision to imprison her on what she knew were fictitious charges. But at the very least she would have wanted to tell him, as his *wife* – not as the queen – she had been devoted to him, that she had loved him and knew he had loved her, and she would never have betrayed him in such an egregious manner.

Might it have made a difference in the dreadful outcome had he known of its message? It's doubtful that Henry would have been moved from his committed intent to marry Jane Seymour. Added to his great disappointment at Anne's failure to produce a son, he had been incited to rage against her by the humiliation of having possibly been cuckolded by his closest friends. His jealousy and fury made him susceptible to any and all impugning suggestions about her. Henry did what Henry most excelled at: he decisively shut out all unpleasantness and insulated himself against guilt and remorse through engaging distractions. And he had a significant distraction at the ready – his wedding. And so he paid scarce attention when the cannon boomed from the Tower signalling Anne's death. His life proceeded, consumed by matters of state and his new bride.

There was joy for Henry when Jane birthed the son he had longed for. The joy was short-lived, though, when Jane died leaving Henry in that most vulnerable state – lonely and unwed. Henry was a man who did not feel comfortable unless he was married, and of course a monarch should have a wife. The problem was that, after Anne, none of his wives fulfilled his expectations. Jane died, Anne of Cleves he considered entirely unsuitable, Catherine Howard betrayed him, driving him into a deep depression over his lost youth and robust health, and finally the saintly Katharine Parr was nursemaid to the shell of the man he had once been.

Henry in his later life is considered by many as a tyrant – oppressive, unnaturally cruel and uncaring, manipulative and impulsive. Certainly, many of his behaviours reflect such a tyrannical nature. It is provocative, though, to consider the possibility that his physical and mental decline may have been aggravated by the guilt and sorrow suffered over his headlong destruction of wives and friends who he had at one time loved profoundly. In his moments alone, when he looked upon his daughter Elizabeth, was he reminded of the young Anne? Did he recognise, in his heart of hearts, those truths which she had expressed to him in her emotional and heart-wrenching final letter?

Whether or not he ever privately acknowledged his own personal pain, it's difficult to imagine there were no residual effects on his psyche after he had witnessed so much tragedy, even for such an egoist.

As his health rapidly waned and his life drew to its end in January 1547, Henry's close friends attended him. Sir Anthony Denny, the writer and religious theorist John Foxe, and perhaps several others quietly moved throughout his chambers providing for his final needs. It was Denny who, at the desperate appeal of the king's physicians, was able to tell Henry that his death was imminent so he might prepare himself. At Henry's request his spiritual leader, the Archbishop of Canterbury, Thomas Cranmer, was summoned. It is said that by the time Cranmer arrived, Henry was unable to speak, but that his faith was confirmed by a squeeze of the archbishop's hand. [34]

---

34   MacCulloch, Diarmaid, *Thomas Cranmer*,
     Yale University Press, 1996, p 360.

In the thirty-six hours prior to his death there were just a few courtiers who saw and spoke with the king. We know that Anthony Denny served him and spoke with him about the most intimate subject, his impending death. What the nature of their conversation was, or other conversations were with the other few gentlemen who were permitted to see Henry in those last hours has not been documented.

But there does exist today a most intriguing and curious written reference, which may at last illuminate the question that desperately begs for an answer: did Henry think of Anne after her death? Did he regret his actions concerning her last days?

The British Library manuscripts collection houses the Lansdowne Catalogue, a series of archives and documents amassed by William Cecil and by the esteemed antiquarian Bishop White Kennett (1660 – 1728). The collection is quite large and consists of groupings of volumes. The volume of interest is entitled *Biographical Memorials* and was the work of Kennett. It's said to be written in his own hand. The book of handwritten entries was produced around 1715 and in a folio labelled 'Original Correspondence' is a page dedicated to the death of Anne Boleyn. On this sheet is a series of seemingly disconnected recordings about Anne's death. Close to the bottom of the thin parchment is written the following inscription:

> The King acknowledges with great griefe at his death the injuries he had done to the Lady Anne Boleyn and her daughter as Thevet in his Cosmogr. lib xvi a writer in no way partial hath testified.

This statement is followed by several lines in old French. What could this mean? Let us examine a modern day transcription of the page:

1536

Memoirs of Queen Anne Boleyn
beheaded 19 May 1536

Some letters relating to the manner of accusing
Queen Anne and the King's departure from her
May 1 1536 and her being sent prisoner to the
Tower

Sententia

Letter of Thomas Archbishop of Canterbury to the
King in a soft and tender vindication of Queen
Anne Prisoner in the Tower dat. 3 May

Her dying speech 19 May

20 May the K married Jane Seymour

This cruelly hindered Melanchthon from thinking
any longer of his intended voyage in to England
____ [the Latin inscription is loosely translated as:
*Philipp Melanchton and Joachimo Camerario date of
journey June 1536 – I am now greatly relieved from
the concern of making travel to England due to the
dire changes there _____ the late Queen who
was more wrongfully accused than convicted and
who paid the ultimate sacrifice]*

In the learned reply to a libel of 16 persons entitled
A Temperate Watchword to [by?] Sir Francis
Hastings Turbulent Watchword [4th gov? p. 58] [35]

The King acknowledges with great griefe at
his death the injuries he had done to the Lady
Anne Boleyn and her daughter as Thevet in his
Cosmogr. lib xvi a writer in no way partial hath
testified. Plusiers Gentilhommes Anglois (says
he speaking of K. Henry's death) /the French
is translated as: *Several English gentlemen have
confided to me that he has repented, upon his
deathbed, of the injustices done to Queen Anne
Boleyn; of her having been falsely accused and for the
punishment imposed upon her; that she died in good
Christian standing and is to be buried in accordance
with the Church of Rome. It is in association with
this ordeal/situation that he (Henri) has attempted to
right these injustices and, with his whole heart, signs
his name to this testimony].*

Afterward, it pleased God to put in the King's
mind to release the [hate?] that barred her Majestie
{Queen Eliz} of her right which he did by his last
will. This to nearly touched the [papists?] that
as it should seem they have abolished it, thereby
endeavouring to take away all monuments and
records whereby her right might be proved.

---

35   Hastings, Sir Francis, *A Watchword to All Religious and True-Hearted
English men,* printed by Felix Kingston for Ralph Iackson, London,
1598, folio 58. Quotation referred to is as follows: "to draw chri|stians
from Gods truth, to his false religion; and to withdraw subiects
from obedience to their lawful So|ueraigne; a worke well beseeming
Antichrist, and all his adherents. Against whom the heathen shall rise
in iudgement, and shall con|demne them; who thought it vn|honest,
and vnhonorable, not one|ly to plot, and deuise treasons, but euen
so much as to hearken to any treason offered them, though ne|uer so
much for their benefit."

The interpretation of this page of writing constitutes a study unto itself.

Certainly, there are clear religious overtones: Kennett was a learned man, a member of the clergy of the Church of England; he quotes a Latin inscription from Philipp Melanchthon, who was a renowned theologian and close friend of Martin Luther. It's apparent that Melanchthon and the German theological scholar Joachim Camerarius planned to travel to England in June 1536 but abandoned their trip after the death of Anne and the marriage of the king to Jane Seymour, whose family represented allegiance to the Catholic Church of Rome. Kennett then chose to refer to writings from Sir Francis Hastings, who was a Puritan, and whose specified passage rails against the plotting and devising of treason.

Kennett next copies a passage from a work written by André Thévet.

Thévet is an intriguing and somewhat enigmatic figure in history. He was born in approximately 1516 in Angoulême, France. He became a Franciscan monk at a relatively young age and, although he never cut ties with the Franciscan order, he commenced an unusual life of worldwide travel and writing. He was prodigious at both, eventually traveling to Asia as well as South America and possibly into North America. Ultimately, he was appointed chaplain for Catherine de Medici. His writings cover the spectrum from botany and biology to theology and cosmology. One of his major works was *Cosmographie Universelle,* published in 1575.[36] In this volume, Thévet includes a significant paragraph that describes information he received about Henry's deathbed grief over Anne and Elizabeth. It is particularly astonishing because, as Kennett states, Thévet would have been a writer "in no way partial" to predetermined views about Anne's culpability.

---

36 Thévet, André, *La Cosmographie Universelle*, Guillaume Chaudiere, Paris, 1575, p 657.

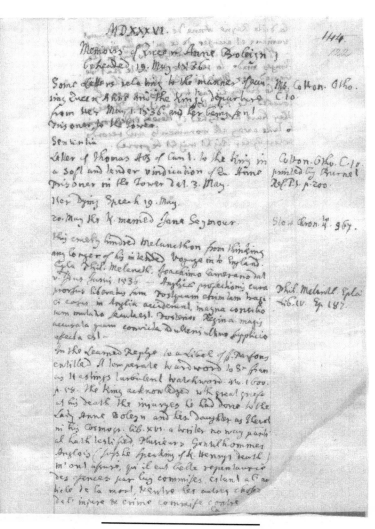

Figure 10 - Lansdowne Document Front
© 01/09/2015 The British Library Board, Lansdowne 979 f122r

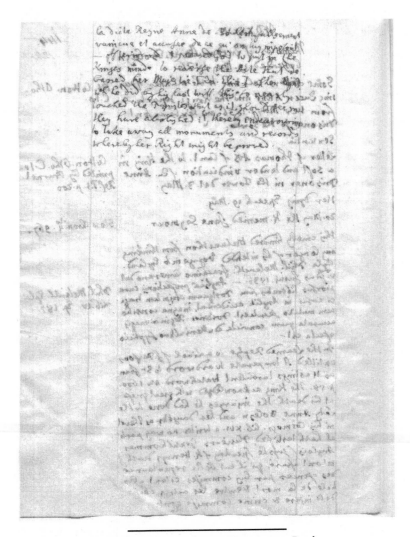

Figure 11 - Lansdowne Document Back
© 01/09/2015 The British Library Board, Lansdowne 979 f122v

One must wonder how a man like Thévet would have come to be told such a thing by "several English gentlemen". In piecing together facts about his life and travels, it is probable that Thévet visited, and likely lived for periods of time, with the Greenwich Franciscan Friars, whose friary was located in a building adjoining the royal Palace of Placentia at Greenwich. This friary figured so significantly in the lives of the English royal family and the nobility that Henry VII and his wife Elizabeth of York provided the friars a large grant, which not only established the convent on the grounds of the palace, but funded its adornment with a major stained glass window. The king left them money in his will for the upkeep of the property and food for the monks. Their second-born son, Henry VIII, was probably christened in the church within the friary proper, and it is very likely that Katharine of Aragon and Henry were married in that same church. It was there, also, that Princess Mary and Princess Elizabeth were christened. Members of the Henrician Court regularly depended upon the friars for spiritual guidance, consultation and confession. Therefore, it is not difficult to imagine that Brother André Thévet, who was thirty-one years of age when Henry VIII died, was well-known to gentlemen of the Court, and perhaps to Henry himself.[37]

The divisive conflicts that arose as a result of the king's desire to divorce Katharine affected the relationship between the Franciscan community and Henry and his advocates. The official position of the Franciscan monks was in distinct opposition to the proposed divorce. There was vocal discord between the king, his allies and the friars. Henry was not happy about the rift, but maintained a sense of restraint, at least for some time. The association between the king and the religious community remained erratic over the years that followed, never being restored to the original closeness that Henry's mother and father had nurtured.

---

37 British History Online, "Friaries: The observant friars of Greenwich",
    in A History of the County of Kent: Volume 2,
    ed. William Page (London, 1926), pp. 194-198.

Figure 12 - Etching of André Thevet, from book 1 of
*Les vrais pourtraits et vies des hommes illustres grecz,
latins et payens,* 1584

Considering the Franciscans were not proponents of Queen Anne Boleyn or her reformist influence, it is even more significant that Thévet would record for posterity that which must have been mentioned only covertly, and to very few individuals at the time – Henry's suffering the great grief of remorse as his death approached, specifically over injuries he had caused Anne. Most extraordinary, the confession does not broadly encompass others who were put to death at Henry's command. According to Thévet's assertion, Henry acknowledged Anne's innocence, regretted the punishment he had invoked, and knew that she had died in good standing with her God.

Henry prepared to meet his creator and hoped, as Anne had declared, that he would be pardoned for his 'great Sin'.

As perhaps an act of repentance, he did restore their daughter Elizabeth to the line of succession.

Did Brother André Thévet, and then Bishop White Kennett, record the truth so history would regard Henry's last hours with a sense of compassion, and to confirm that Anne's innocence will forever be known and remembered?

That, gentle reader, is for you to decide.

Figure 13 - Franciscan Friary Greenwich adjoining Placentia

AFTERWORD
Anne's letter: the legacy

What has been the heritage of this wonderful letter since it became the property of Sir Robert Cotton?

As mentioned, his entire collection was left to Cotton's son, then his grandson, for safekeeping and preservation. In its early years as a noted collection of national importance, it was stored in Cotton House. As years wore on, it became obvious that the private home was not a suitable place for such an amassed treasure (the library contained Cotton's pride and joy, the fifth-century Greek Genesis – Otho B. VI – one of the earliest illustrated Christian manuscripts in existence; it included the original, single medieval manuscript of Beowulf – nearly 1,000 years old; two of the four surviving letters patent of King John recording the grant of Magna Carta – Cotton Charter XIII. 31a – and the only one that had the Great Seal still attached; the bull confirming the title 'Defender of the Faith' on Henry VIII – now Vitellius B. IV ; as well as the letters from Kingston and Anne Boleyn, in addition to many other priceless artefacts). The architect Sir Christopher Wren surveyed the structure and pronounced it subject to almost complete demolishing and rebuilding. He proposed that the library be moved to a space in the House of Lords. However, some questionable financial manoeuvrings by those involved in the decision-making led to sinking over £4,500, a massive sum at the time, into renovations at Cotton House. Nonetheless, the space was still unsuitable, being located close to the river that pervaded the rooms with a dampness that was rapidly causing the books' and papers' destruction. It was necessary to keep fires burning at all times to ward off the damp, even though it was recognised this also caused a hazard.

Finally, in 1729, a possibility arose to move the collection to a mansion called Ashburnam House in Westminster. The location was an interesting choice, since the building was originally a part of a medieval monastery, one that had been closed in the Dissolution of Monasteries, and it was a building well-known to Robert Cotton because it was adjacent to Westminster School, where he had studied antiquary science under the tutelage of William Camden. The entire library was thereby moved and situated in its new home in Westminster.

On Friday 22 October 22 1731, the residents of Ashburnam House retired for the night. By 2 am, they were awakened by a thick haze of smoke and sent an emergency call to the fire brigade. They, and other neighbours, made heroic efforts to save as much of the library as they could, desperately throwing books of medieval illumination, early recorded bibles, codexes and letters from the windows. In the meantime, the fire company had begun to stream water on the building, which doused the surrounding books and papers lying smouldering in the street. In the aftermath of the fire the devastation was painful to observe. The house was reduced to rubble and in the courtyard were sodden lumps of precious documents, those that were merely ash lay all about like wet, grey snow. It was called the greatest disaster of bibliographic materials in England's history.[38]

Once as many fragments as possible had been gathered and consolidated, the supervision of the damaged library's disposition was handled by Speaker Arthur Onslow. Onslow was a trustee of the library and had been one of the individuals who bravely entered the burning house to save as much of the precious collection as was possible. It was Onslow who put together a

---

38   Prescott, Andrew, "Their Present Miserable State of Cremation: the Restoration of the Cotton Library", an essay from *Sir Robert Cotton as Collector: Essays on an Early Stuart Courtier and His Legacy*, edited by C. J. Wright, London, British Library Publications, 1997, pp 391-454.

group of experts, including specialists from the Chapter House at Westminster, the Tower of London, as well as the exchequer. It was their job to determine how the damaged manuscripts might be conserved. Parchments that had been soaked with water needed to be stretched and dried – some by air – others that were too wet, near a fire, under close supervision. Some volumes that were comprised of sheets of vellum had actually been fused shut. The heat of the fire caused the fat and collagen in the animal skins of the vellum to melt. When cooled, they had congealed to a solid mass. These books needed specific care to re-open and restore. It was a daunting and massive job. Using early and somewhat awkward methods, the committee of specialists and craftspeople did a remarkable job. However, many of the documents and books remain as mere fragments of what they had been and today there is an entire compendium of small shreds that remain in drawers in the British Library. Perhaps future conservators may be able to progress the salvage efforts that took place over 250 years ago.[39]

One of the catalogues that sustained a great deal of damage was the Otho collection. Anne's letter, as well as those of William Kingston, were part of this grouping. It is miraculous that these letters survive. It is also fortuitous that the letters were copied prior to the fire. It's only due to these copies that we have a full disclosure of the letters' contents.

Most of the study and analysis of Anne's letter has been taken from printed copies, as published by various historians and authors. It's evident that many, if not most people who have commented on its authenticity and provenance, have not seen the original, or even an image of the original, both front and back. Those images are reproduced in this book so they can afford a close scrutiny by the reader.

Since the eighteenth and nineteenth centuries, who has written about this important testimony signed by Anne Boleyn?

---

39   Kuhns, Matt, *Cotton's Library: The Many Perils of Preserving History*, Lyon Hall Press, Ohio, 2014.

Modern-day historians and authors refer to the authenticity of the letter with a level of controversy equivalent to their predecessors. Jasper Ridley, in his biography *Henry VIII, The Politics of Tyranny*, states: "The letter which she is supposed to have written to Henry is a forgery, written in the reign of her daughter, Elizabeth."[40] Subsequently, Ridley reversed his opinion, as mentioned in his book *The Love Letters of Henry VIII.* [41]

The renowned biographer of Anne Boleyn, Professor Eric Ives, deals with the letter in this way: "It would appear to be wholly improbable for Anne to write that her marriage was built on nothing but the King's fancy and that her incarceration was the consequence of Henry's affection for Jane. Equally it would have been totally counterproductive for a Tudor prisoner in the Tower to warn the King, as the letter does, that he is in imminent danger of the judgement of God!"[42]

Alison Weir's work, *The Lady In the Tower*, devotes over four pages to the subject of the letter.[43] In them she poses various questions about aspects of the letter and its history that have proved confusing. She offers arguments both for and against its credibility, citing observations made by historians early and modern. It seems that a particular point of dissension is the fact that Anne's name is spelled variously from the typical "Boleyn", and that she referred to herself using her given name rather than as queen. Another stated difference is the observation that the handwriting is evidently not Anne's. Additionally, Weir makes mention that the historian John Strype claimed to have seen another letter written by Anne in the Tower – in which Anne

---

40   Ridley, Jasper, *Henry VIII The Politics of Tyranny*, Viking, New York, 1985, p 269.

41   Ridley, Jasper, ed., *The Love Letters of Henry VIII*, Weidenfeld Nicolson, 1989.

42   Ives, E., *Life and Death of Anne Boleyn*, p 58.

43   Weir, Alison, *The Lady in the Tower*, Random House, 2010, pp 178-183.

responds again to the demand for a full confession. In actuality, this response is recorded on the reverse of the original document, albeit not in Anne's personal handwriting.

Other Tudor author-historians, including David Starkey, Suzannah Lipscomb, David Loades, Antonia Fraser and Retha Warnicke, omit any discussion of the letter at all.

In a recent book written by Susan Bordo, *The Creation of Anne Boleyn*, the author compares the elegant style of the letter to the equally poignant speech purportedly delivered by Anne at her sentencing. Bordo makes note of the probability that the letter found in Cromwell's papers was never delivered to the king. She recognises that the letter may be authentic, having been scribed by a hand other than Anne's, and significantly, observes the intimacy and personal sentiment expressed in the first line of a letter composed from wife to husband. She recognises, with insight, and remarks upon the powerful single-mindedness of a woman who fully intended to express her last thoughts to a man she had loved profoundly, lived with, and for whom she had borne a child.[44]

As part of the enduring legend of Anne Boleyn and Henry VIII, mysteries abound. How their lives, passionately and fatefully entwined, could have disjoined so murderously is an abiding question that has, and will continue to, evoke study and reflection.

Two seemingly small details in the grand scheme of Henry and Anne's time together: the letter "from my doleful Prison in the Tower this 6 May", and the statement "The King acknowledges with great griefe at his death the injuries he had done to the Lady Anne Boleyn" may be far more momentous than previously known or considered.

With thoughtful scrutiny and additional research, these traces of the past may provide us with some of the answers we seek.

---

44   Bordo, Susan, *The Creation of Anne Boleyn*, Mariner Books, 2013, pp 109-112.

History and time line of Anne's Tower Letter

Letter's creation at the Tower of London

Author: **Anne Boleyn** -------------- composed
(Scribe: Unknown)   6 May 1536

Ralph Sadler ---------------- received letter
personal secretary to Thomas Cromwell   c.7-8 May 1536

Thomas Cromwell ------------- handed letter
Henry VIII's chief counsellor   c.7-8 May, 1536

Letter hidden with -------------- hidden from
Cromwell's private papers   1536-1540

Cromwell's beheading --------------28 July 1540

Ralph Sadler retrieves letter ------------ July 1540

William Cecil, Lord Burghley--------given letter by Sadler
chief advisor to Elizabeth   c. 1540-1550

Queen Elizabeth I (and Lord Burghley)--------- c. 1550-1600
in possession of letter

William Camden, antiquarian -------- inherits letter from
Burghley c. 1580-1598

Sir Robert Bruce Cotton ---------- inherits letter from
antiquarian and collector of manuscripts   Camden
c. 1623

Sir Thomas and **Sir John Cotton**, --------library inherited
son and grandson   1631

Sir John Cotton, grandson and custodian ----- maintain library
of Cotton manuscripts   until c. 1700

Ashburnam House fire destroys -------- letter damaged
Cotton Library documents   October 1731

British Museum library possession -------- 1732 - present
and restoration of 'The Tower Letter'

Resources

Bordo, Susan, *The Creation of Anne Boleyn*, Mariner Books, 2013

British History Online, "Friaries: The observant friars of Greenwich", in *A History of the County of Kent: Volume 2*, ed. William Page, London, 1926

British Library: Stowe MS 151; Cotton MS Otho CX; Lansdowne 979

British Library Online, "Explore Archives and Manuscripts", http://www.bl.uk/catalogues/manuscripts/primo_library/libweb

Burnet, Gilbert, *Historie of the Reformation of the Church of England*, Part One, London, 1679

Cabala, Sive Scrinia Sacra, Mysteries of State and Government in Letters, Temple Gate, 1663

Calendar of State Papers Foreign and Domestic, of the Reign of Henry VIII, ed. Brewer, Gairdner, Brodie, 1862 – 1932

Camden Miscellany, Volume 39, Offices of the Royal Historical Society, London, 1990

Camden, William, *Historie of the Most Renowned and Victorious Princesse Elizabeth Late Queen of England*, Benjamin Fisher, London, 1630

Cassell's Illustrated History of England Vol II, Cassell & Company Limited

Cavendish, George, *The Life of Thomas Wolsey*, ed. Ellis, F. S., Kelmscott Press, London, 1893

Ellis, Henry, *Original Letters, Illustrative of English History*,

Vol II, Thomas Davison, Whitefriars, London 1815

Elton, G. R., *Reform and Renewal: Thomas Cromwell and the Common Weal*; University of Chicago Press Cambridge, 1974

Flannagan, Roy, "Review of In Praise of Scribes", Early Modern Literary Studies 5.1, May 1999

Froude, James, *History of England from the Fall of Wolsey to the Death of Elizabeth*, Vol II, Scribner, New York, 1872

Hastings, Sir Francis, *A Watchword to All Religious and True-Hearted English men*, printed by Felix Kingston for Ralph Jackson, London, 1598

Ives, Eric, *The Life and Death of Anne Boleyn*, Blackwell Publishing, Oxford, UK, 2004

Keynes, Simon, "The Reconstruction of a Burnt Cottonian Manuscript", British Library articles: www.bl.uk, 1996

Kuhns, Matt, *Cotton's Library: The Many Perils of Preserving History*, Lyon Hall Press, Ohio, 2014

Latymer, William, *Cronickille of Anne Bulleyne*, Camden Miscellany Vol 39, Royal Historical Society, 1990

Lord Herbert of Cherbury, *The Life and Raigne of King Henry the Eighth*, Thomas Whitaker, London, 1649

MacCulloch, Diarmaid, *Thomas Cranmer*, Yale University Press, 1996

Nares, Edward, *Memoirs of the Life and Administration of the Right Honourable William Cecil, Lord Burghley*, Saunders and Otley, London, 1828

Parker, T. M., "Was Thomas Cromwell a Machiavellian?" The Journal of Ecclesiastical History, Volume 1, Issue 01, Cambridge University Press, 25 Mar 2011

Prescott, Andrew, "Their Present Miserable State of Cremation: the Restoration of the Cotton Library" an essay from *Sir Robert Cotton as Collector: Essays on an Early Stuart Courtier and His Legacy*, edited by C. J. Wright, London,

British Library Publications, 1997

Richardson, R. C., "William Camden and the Re-Discovery of England", Trans. Leicestershire Archeological and Historical Society, 2004

Ridgway, Claire, *The Fall of Anne Boleyn: A Countdown*, MadeGlobal Publishing, 2012

Ridley, Jasper, ed., *The Love Letters of Henry VIII*, Weidenfeld Nicolson, 1989

Ridley, Jasper, *Henry VIII The Politics of Tyranny*, Viking, New York, 1985

Strickland, Agnes, *Lives of the Queens of England*, Vols 4 and 5, Lea and Blanchard, 1851

Strype, John, *Ecclesiastical Memorials Under the Reign of King Henry VIII King Edward VI and Queen Mary I*, Vol I, 1816

Thévet, André, *La Cosmographie Universelle*, Guillaume Chaudiere, Paris, 1575

Thrush, A. and Ferris, J. ed., *The History of Parliament: the House of Commons 1604-1629*, Cambridge University Press, 2010

Weir, Alison, *The Lady in the Tower*, Random House, 2010

List of Figures

Sandra Vasoli, author of *Anne Boleyn's Letter from the Tower*, earned a Bachelor's degree in English and biology from Villanova University before embarking on a thirty-five-year career in human resources for a large international company.

Having written essays, stories, and articles all her life, Vasoli was prompted by her overwhelming fascination with the Tudor dynasty to try her hand at writing both historical fiction and non-fiction. While researching what would eventually become her *Je Anne Boleyn series*, Vasoli was granted unprecedented access to the Papal Library. There she was able to read the original love letters from Henry VIII to Anne Boleyn—an event that contributed greatly to her research and writing.

Vasoli currently lives in Gwynedd Valley, Pennsylvania, with her husband and two greyhounds.

MadeGlobal Publishing

Non-Fiction History

- Jasper Tudor - **Debra Bayani**
- Illustrated Kings and Queens of England - **Claire Ridgway**
- A History of the English Monarchy - **Gareth Russell**
- The Fall of Anne Boleyn - **Claire Ridgway**
- George Boleyn: Tudor Poet, Courtier & Diplomat - **Ridgway & Cherry**
- The Anne Boleyn Collection - **Claire Ridgway**
- The Anne Boleyn Collection II - **Claire Ridgway**
- Sweating Sickness in a Nutshell - **Claire Ridgway**
- Mary Boleyn in a Nutshell - **Sarah Bryson**
- Thomas Cranmer in a Nutshell - **Beth von Staats**
- On This Day in Tudor History - **Claire Ridgway**
- Two Gentleman Poets at the Court of Henry VIII - **Edmond Bapst**
- A Mountain Road - **Douglas Weddell Thompson**

Historical Fiction

- Phoenix Rising - **Hunter S. Jones**
- Cor Rotto - **Adrienne Dillard**
- The Claimant - **Simon Anderson**
- The Truth of the Line - **Melanie V. Taylor**
- The Merry Wives of Henry VIII - **Ann Nonny**

Other Books

- Easy Alternate Day Fasting - **Beth Christian**
- 100 Under 500 Calorie Meals - **Beth Christian**
- 100 Under 200 Calorie Desserts - **Beth Christian**
- 100 Under 500 Calorie Vegetarian Meals - **Beth Christian**
- Interviews with Indie Authors - **Claire Ridgway**
- Popular - **Gareth Russell**
- The Immaculate Deception - **Gareth Russell**
- The Walls of Truth - **Melanie V. Taylor**
- Talia's Adventures - **Verity Ridgway**
- Las Aventuras de Talia (Spanish) - **Verity Ridgway**

Please Leave a Review

If you enjoyed this book, *please* leave a review at the book seller where you purchased it. There is no better way to thank the author and it really does make a huge difference! *Thank you in advance.*

Made in the USA
San Bernardino, CA
02 March 2017